HORSES!

A MY INCREDIBLE WORLD PICTURE BOOK

MY INCREDIBLE WORLD

Copyright © 2018, My Incredible World

All rights reserved. This book or any portion thereof may not be reproduced or used in any manner whatsoever without the express written permission of the copyright holder.

www.myincredibleworld.com

Photos Credits
Cover photo by Helena Lopes, available at https://unsplash.com/photos/Y5iPU37b7Zs
Page 1.   Untitled by Christine Mendoza, available at https://unsplash.com/photos/HDDZOfX8pLA
Page 2.   Untitled by Kym Ellis, available at https://unsplash.com/photos/_c8lBqTRIEc
Page 3.   Untitled by Oscar Nilsson, available at https://unsplash.com/photos/-Ylz_tc8NOk
Page 4.   Untitled by osker wyld, available at https://unsplash.com/photos/O6gkt5cwFNk
Page 5.   Untitled by Rich Dahlgren, available at https://unsplash.com/photos/-MMRAIrqgUE
Page 6.   Untitled by Natasha Bhogal, available at https://unsplash.com/photos/Ca_8QR9BZpU
Page 7.   Untitled by Ryan Waring, available at https://unsplash.com/photos/6T7GCuh_C0c
Page 8.   Untitled by Tanja Heffner, available at https://unsplash.com/photos/Fx-WC4Z8nSo
Page 9.   Untitled by Lisa Lyne Blevins, available at https://unsplash.com/photos/6OdJ4qIwL0s
Page 10. Untitled by Thomas Peham, available at https://unsplash.com/photos/7UTgWorEKEI
Page 11. Untitled by Josephine Amalie Paysen, available at https://unsplash.com/photos/MCtaCBqxLxY
Page 12. Untitled by Cristy Zinn, available at https://unsplash.com/photos/hqxxhnrSnwE
Page 13. Untitled by Gene Devine, available at https://unsplash.com/photos/ahxNfsInPVM
Page 14. Untitled by timothy muza, available at https://unsplash.com/photos/4F42IqLRjf4
Page 15. Untitled by Annie Spratt, available at https://unsplash.com/photos/qem7xLMt1bU
Page 16. Untitled by Gabriela Kucerova, available at https://unsplash.com/photos/j3NQl-B0R1U
Page 17. Untitled by Annie Spratt, available at https://unsplash.com/photos/GdLACbcQwwg
Page 18. Untitled by Daniel Apodaca, available at https://unsplash.com/photos/bOp9iPHzkjM
Page 19. Untitled by Soledad Lorieto, available at https://unsplash.com/photos/bSQ2YL5tytY
Page 20. Untitled by Paz Arando, available at https://unsplash.com/photos/ISf-Z96VRk4
Page 21. Untitled by Siarhei Plashchynski, available at https://unsplash.com/photos/6qV4kFs9npg
Page 22. Untitled by Thomas Tucker, available at https://unsplash.com/photos/-CERq9zVku4

Horses live all over the world except in northern Arctic regions.

There are about 60 million horses on the planet and over 300 breeds!

Horses have a variety of different coat colors and patterns.

Horses are **grazing** animals and eat mostly grasses and hay.

Horses drink up to 10 gallons (38 L) of water every day!

Horses have excellent hearing and can move their ears 180 degrees!

Horses only see limited colors but they have panoramic vision!

Horses have extraordinary balance!

Horses can sleep lying down or standing up!

Horse hooves never stop growing!

Horses usually live to be 25 to 30 years old.

Horses can **walk**, **trot**, **gallop** and **jump**.

Horses can gallop at almost 30 miles per hour (48 km/h). That's fast!

Horses can weigh between 840 and 2,200 pounds (380 - 1000 kg)!

A **pony** is a small breed of horse.

Horses can communicate by **neighing** and **whinnying**.

Horses are intelligent and clever.

Horses were once a major form of transportation for humans.

A baby horse is called a **foal**.

A baby horse can stand up and run shortly after it is born!

Horses are social animals that like to live in a group.

Horses are incredible!

Made in United States
Troutdale, OR
09/26/2024